7 STEPS TO LAUNCHING YOUR PODCAST

Plan, Record, and Publish

DR. TINA J. RAMSAY

7 STEPS TO LAUNCHING YOUR PODCAST

Affiliate Disclosure

Links marked (A) are affiliate links. Purchasing through them never costs you extra and helps me continue producing free resources for the community.

General Disclaimer

This book is for educational purposes only. The author and publisher are not liable for any damages or losses allegedly caused directly or indirectly by the information contained herein. Always conduct your own due diligence and seek professional advice where appropriate.

Dedication

To my Heavenly Father—thank You for ordering my steps, reminding me that "there is nothing new under the sun," and proving that when we "seek first the Kingdom," everything we need is added. May this book make a lasting impact for Your glory.

To every coach and mentor who poured into me—thank you.

To my family—Curtis, our amazing children, and my loving parents—thank you for being my unwavering security and support. I love you deeply.

To our loyal CTR Nation listeners, readers, and referral partners—your faithfulness fuels the mission.

To our valued sponsors, clients, and customers—thank you for believing in purpose-driven media.

To the entire CTR Fam—our podcasters and TV hosts—thank you for amplifying hope to 350 million households in 140 countries.

And finally, to you, the reader: your voice truly matters. When you launch your podcast, you'll change the world for the better.

— Dr. Tina J Ramsay

Introduction

Hello-hello, everybody!

I'm Dr. Tina J Ramsay.

Yes, I wrote the 200-page 5X award winning bestseller ***The Power of Podcasting: Unlocking Tips & Strategies for Podcast Success,*** but after coaching hundreds of podcasters I discovered one hard truth:

Less reading, more action = faster results.

That's why you're holding this **bite-size playbook**. In seven laser-focused steps you'll move from idea to live episode—checking boxes, seeing progress, and staying motivated. **Drop the excuses:** if you're reading this, you already know you have something the world needs to hear.

Use these simple action steps, **tag @CTRMediaNetwork** when you launch, and let's celebrate your voice going global.

Happy Podcasting!
Dr. Tina J Ramsay, (h.c)

Table of Contents

How to Use This Playbook

- **This book is designed to help you** plan, record, and publish your podcast fast.
- **Each step features a motivating scripture and affirmation** to keep you inspired.
- **You will need** a notebook and pen to answer the questions.
- **Take one step at a time**—finish the checklist, then move on.
- **Scan the QR codes** for resources and signup links.
- **Affiliate links** (A) never cost you extra and help fund our free community resources.

Ready? Let's go!

STEP 1 — PODCAST WITH A PURPOSE

Why this step matters

Verse: "Commit to the Lord whatever you do, and He will establish your plans." — Proverbs 16:3

Affirmation: I commit my podcast to God's purpose, trusting Him to establish every step.

Purpose is your fuel. When downloads dip or life gets busy, a crystal-clear why keeps you pressing record. Nail the mission now, and every future decision—from guests to monetization—stays aligned.

Five Clarity Questions

1 Why do you want to start a podcast?
2 What will it be about?
3 Who is it for?
4 How will listening help them?
5 When will you launch?

DO-IT-NOW CHECKLIST

☐ Write a one-sentence mission.
☐ List three problems you'll solve.
☐ Circle a launch date on a calendar.

STEP 2 —
NAME YOUR PODCAST

Why this step matters

Verse: "A good name is more desirable than great riches." — Proverbs 22:1

Affirmation: I choose a clear, memorable name that reflects my mission and honors my brand.

Your title is your podcast's first handshake with the world. A clear, on-brand name plus locked-in digital real estate prevents confusion, protects your brand, and positions you as a pro from day one.

Best-Practice Reminders

- Be creative
- Match your brand
- Use descriptive keywords

DO-IT-NOW CHECKLIST

☐ Brainstorm five names → search Apple/Spotify for duplicates.
☐ Pick the easiest-to-spell option.
☐ Claim your show name on FB, IG, YT, LinkedIn, TikTok.
☐ Create a Google Business Profile so your podcast appears on Google Maps.
☐ Set up a dedicated podcast e-mail (e.g., info@showname.com).
☐ Decide on show style: Solo or Guest-Driven
☐ If Guest-Driven, plan to use the CTR Partner Platform in Podcast Tips, Strategies, Tools, and checklists for vetted guests at the back of this book.

STEP 3 —
KNOW YOUR LISTENERS

Why this step matters

Verse: "Each of you should use whatever gift you have received to serve others." — 1 Peter 4:10

Affirmation: I listen first so I can serve my audience with excellence.

You don't create episodes for "everyone." Defining a listener avatar ensures every topic, guest, and promo speaks directly to the people most likely to binge—and share—your show.

The Avatar-Building Four Template

1 Age range?
2 Job/business?
3 Biggest struggles?
4 Why they listen to you?

DO-IT-NOW CHECKLIST

□ Complete the Avatar template.
□ Write a show intro that speaks to that avatar.
□ List three podcasts your avatar already loves (spot your market gap).

STEP 4 — DESCRIBE YOUR PODCAST

Why this step matters

Verse: "Write the vision; make it plain on tablets, so he may run who reads it." — Habakkuk 2:2

Affirmation: I communicate my podcast's value with clarity and confidence.

A tight show description does the heavy lifting when you're not in the room—inside podcast apps, pitch emails, and sponsor decks. Pre-planning episode titles and numbering keeps you consistent and shows listeners you're serious.

Key Questions

1. Who is your podcast for?
2. Why are you creating this podcast?
3. What problems will your podcast solve?
4. When and what day will your podcast air each, week?
5. Where can the audience listen to your podcast?

- Set audience expectations.
- Double Check Spelling and Grammar

DO-IT-NOW CHECKLIST

☐ Draft a 150-character audience blurb.
☐ Draft a 75-word guest blurb.
☐ Check spelling & grammar.
☐ Add a "What to Expect" bullet list.
☐ Outline titles for your first 3–4 episodes to launch with a mini-arc.
☐ Write a one-sentence description for each episode.
☐ Choose an episode-numbering system ("Ep 1") and decide whether to group by Seasons—episode counts motivate you and impress listeners.

STEP 5 —
DESIGN YOUR COVER ART (YOUR PODCAST LOGO)

Why this step matters

Verse: "Let your light shine before others, that they may see your good works." — Matthew 5:16

Affirmation: My podcast visuals boldly shine the message God placed in me.

Professional, readable cover art stops the scroll and communicates quality before a single word is heard. Matching episode graphics keep your brand cohesive across every platform.

Visual Rules

Name crystal-clear, Genre, and Topics

- Keep it Simple
- Ensure It's Easy to Read (no cursive)
- Use Fewer Words
- Use No More Than 3 or 4 Colors
- Use No More than 2 or 3 Fonts

DO-IT-NOW CHECKLIST

☐ Open Free Canva Account→ 3000 × 3000 px template and 500 x 500 template size

☐ Drop show name big & centered; add one visual cue.

☐ Export file format JPEG.

☐ Create two Canva templates:

– Guest Feature Card (logo + guest photo + episode title)

– Solo/Topic Card (logo + host photo + topic headline)

STEP 6 — CHOOSE YOUR TECHNOLOGY & SOFTWARE

Why this step matters

Verse: "Let all things be done decently and in order." — 1 Corinthians 14:40

Affirmation: I steward my resources wisely and keep my production process in order.

Great content can't rescue bad audio or lost files. A lean, organized tech stack ensures you sound clear, record safely, and repurpose efficiently—without breaking the bank.

Starter Tech Stack
• Cell phone
• USB mic
• USB camera (optional)
• Earbuds
• Ring light
• Tripod
• StreamYard for cloud recording (14-day free trial)
• Intro/outro video (Canva or StreamYard)
• One-page website (host link)

DO-IT-NOW CHECKLIST
□ Sign up for StreamYard → (A).
□ Toggle "Local Record" for separate audio/video tracks.
□ Create a 5–15 sec intro/outro video
□ Run a 10-sec room-tone test.
□ Name every file "episodename.wav" (or .mp4) to stay organized.
□ Save recordings to a cloud folder.
□ Build your podcast website in just 5 minutes with CTR Partnered Platform → (A); embed your player for instant SEO.

STEP 7 —
HOST, DISTRIBUTE & JOIN CTR MEDIA NETWORK

Why this step matters

Verse: "Go into all the world and proclaim the good news to all creation."
— Mark 16:15

Affirmation: My podcast reaches the world, amplifying voices and positive impact.

Publishing is only half the battle—distribution, analytics, reviews, and community turn a hobby into real impact. Partnering with CTR Media Network unlocks global reach and ongoing mentorship so that you will never experience podfade.

1 Choose a Hosting Site

• Spreaker (paid)
• Spotify for Creators (free)
• Podbean (paid)
• Buzzsprout (paid)

2 Launch Your Website

Embed your player so each episode auto-updates for SEO.

3 Super-Charge Visibility

• Claim your free CTR Podcast Directory listing.
• Upgrade to CTR membership to stream on Android TV, Amazon Fire TV, Roku, Apple TV & reach 350 million households in 140 countries, plus coaching & community.
• For Guest-Driven/Hybrid shows, join CTR Partner Platform for vetted guests.

DO-IT-NOW CHECKLIST

☐ Upload Episode 1 to your host.
☐ Submit RSS to Apple & Spotify.
☐ Claim free Directory listing
☐ Review & Join CTR membership program
☐ Join CTR Partner Guesting Platform
☐ Track first-week downloads or views on social media in your host dashboard.
☐ Ask listeners to rate & review on Apple Podcasts—early reviews boost discoverability.

PLAN
YOUR PODCAST

FOUR-WEEK PODCAST PLANNING CALENDAR

Use this template to plan your upcoming podcast episodes. Start planning at least 4 weeks in advance to allow time for any mishaps or interruptions.

Week 1: Topic & Guest Selection

- Brainstorm topics for the next couple of episodes.
- Research the latest information surrounding the topic.
- Locate and send out guest invitations. (if applicable)
- Research products / services to promote via affiliate link.

Week 2: Testing & Prep

- Schedule guest speaker. (if applicable)
- Create questions for the guest speaker (if applicable)
- Outline the show, including stories you want to share, which products to promote, etc.
- Test audio, video, lighting, and recording equipment.
- Gather affiliate links to items you will be promoting & create short links that are easy to remember.
- Start talking about the show topic - not necessarily the show itself. Perhaps about the issue the show is going to address (to get the topic on their mind)

Week 3 Record & Edit

- Record & Edit (If needed)
- Record episode
- Follow up to thank the guest for joining you. (if applicable)
- Edit show recording or send to an editor.
- Add intro, background music, and final promos to get the guest and your business. (If needed)
- Create and release pre-launch marketing material, promo flyer, including topic hints, teasers, hyping up your guest speaker, etc.
- If you're doing a live call, send last minute reminders to join you starting 3 hours before the call, 1 hour prior, 10 minutes prior. Use social media and email.
- Get Guest Release Signed

Week 4 Publish & Promote

- Publish according to schedule.
- Test to make sure it's playing correctly on a variety of browsers and devices.
- Distributed throughout all platforms.
- Update descriptions and rewrite pre-launch promos to send post-launch.
- Promote it across all your platforms.
- Track your results. How many joined, how many new subscribers, how many watched the replay, etc?
- Make notes of any changes you want to make before the next episode.
- Make notes of potential new show topics based on the conversation and feedback about this episode.
- Add your Podcast to CTR Media Network for Podcast Distribution and TV to maximize Visibility.

RECORD YOUR PODCAST

STREAMYARD QUICKSTART: RECORD, EDIT & GO LIVE

Let's get you on StreamYard—your all-in-one cloud studio for audio & video.

Grab Your Free Trial

☐ Scan QR code → Activate your 14-day StreamYard trial (A)

PODCAST STREAMYARD STREAMING 14 DAY FREE TRIAL

SCAN

Learn the Interface

☐ Scan QR Code → Watch the "Record, Edit & Publish with StreamYard" tutorial

FILM, EDIT, AND PUBLISH YOUR PODCAST VIDEOS WITH STREAMYARD!

SCAN

Record Your First Session

In StreamYard, enable Local Record to capture separate audio & video tracks

HOW TO GO LIVE WITH STREAMYARD |COMPLETE TUTORIAL

SCAN

Hit **"Go Live"** (you can mark it unlisted if you're practicing) and **press Record**

Quick File Management

☐ Name your files like 2025-07-XX_Ep-001 (or .mp4) immediately after recording

☐ Upload raw files to your cloud folder for safe backup

Edit & Publish

☐ Use StreamYard's built-in trimming tools, or import into your editor of choice

☐ Export a final video file, upload to YouTube or your host, and publish

☐ Upload edited files to Podcast Hosting site such as Spotify for Creators, Spreaker, etc

Keep this guide handy every time you record—

PUBLISH YOUR PODCAST

Quick Publish Podcast Playbook

Now that you've recorded and edited your show in StreamYard, here's the exact process to get your episode live—audio and video—without overwhelm:

1. **Download Your Episode from Streamyard**
   - Choose MP3 (audio only) or MP4 (video + audio) in StreamYard's export menu.
   - Save the file as epiosodename.mp3 (or .mp4) in your podcast folder.

-

2. **Upload to Your Podcast Host**
   - Log in to your preferred podcast host (Spotify for Podcasters, Buzzsprout, Podbean, etc.).
   - Click New Episode (or Upload), select your MP3/MP4 file, and fill in title, description, and cover art aka logo.
   - Hit Publish—your host's RSS feed will automatically push to Apple, Google, Spotify, and 10+ directories.

-

3. **Leverage CTR Media Network Premium Distribution**
   - As a CTR Premium member, simply send us your final MP3/MP4.
   - We'll distribute your video to Amazon Fire TV, Roku, Android TV, Apple TV, iOS app, and Google Play web app—so you don't have to lift a finger.

-

4. **DIY Spotify Walk-Through**
   - Want to handle hosting yourself on Spotify?
   - Scan QR on the next page for a step-by-step video that walks you through setting up, uploading, and optimizing your first episode on Spotify for Podcasters.

DO-IT-NOW CHECKLIST

□ Add your podcast to CTR Podcast Directory

□ Repeat these steps to add additional episodes

□ Post your podcast on social media and send out an email

Congratulations—your show is now live across every major audio and video platform! You are an official podcaster.

How to Start
a Podcast
from Scratch
on
Spotify
SCAN ME
FREE GIFT 31

Final Blessing & Charge

"Now to Him who is able to do exceedingly abundantly above all that we ask or think..."
— Ephesians 3:20

You've walked through the seven steps, filled in the worksheets, and felt the spark of possibility ignite. My prayer is that you never let perfection delay your purpose. Your first episode won't be flawless—but it will be faithful, and that's what the world needs to hear. So, take a deep breath, hit publish, and remember: Your voice matters. Be seen, be heard, be purpose-driven.

Declaration of Intent

I, ________________________**[Reader Name]**, declare that from this moment forward I will:

- **Commit my voice to purpose**—sharing insights, stories, and solutions that uplift and inspire
- **Plan with clarity,** using these seven steps as my roadmap from idea to live episode.
- **Record with confidence,** trusting in the tools, tutorials, and checklists provided here.
- **Publish without fear,** knowing that perfect is the enemy of done and progress fuels momentum.
- **Honor my "why"** each time I press record, anchoring my podcast in the mission God has placed in my heart.
- **Engage with my community,** celebrating every download, review, and listener conversation as a step toward greater impact.
- **Persist through challenges,** letting each obstacle refine my craft rather than derail my dream.

By this declaration, I stake my commitment to becoming a purpose-driven podcaster—leveraging faith, focus, and these seven actionable steps to launch my show, amplify my message, and change the world, one episode at a time.

Signed,

____

PODCAST TIPS, STRATEGIES, TOOLS, AND CHECKLISTS

MARKETING & MEDIA TOOLS

CTR PARTNER GUESTING PLATFORM

SCAN

THE EASIEST WAY TO LIVE STREAM AND RECORD YOUR PODCAST

SCAN

HOW TO CREATE PODCAST LOGO IN CANVA

SCAN

MARKETING & MEDIA TOOLS

BUILD YOUR PODCAST WEBSITE IN JUST 5 MINUTES WITH CTR PARTNERED PLATFORM

SCAN

TURNS LONG VIDEOS INTO SHORTS WITH ONE CLICK

SCAN

Podcast Engagement Checklist

Audience size gets the headlines, but engagement closes the advertising deals and turns a “good” show into a great show. Brands—and savvy listeners—want proof that people aren’t just downloading; they’re leaning in, talking back, and taking action.

- [ ] Keeping your audience engaged is just as important as the content you provide.
- [ ] Make it easy for listeners to contact you. Dedicate an email specifically for your show.
- [ ] Encourage listeners to reach out to you with their comments and questions.
- [ ] Respond to their emails, DMs and messages as quickly as possible. You don't have to have long, drawn out conversations, but do answer their initial question.
- [ ] Answer listener questions in your podcast episodes.
- [ ] Remember your regulars and something special about them. Address them by name and point out what you remember, or ask about it, etc. Recognition boosts engagement.
- [ ] Talk about the feedback you've received from a customer and ask if others have experienced something similar.
- [ ] Share a story about the success of a listener, customer, or follower.
- [ ] Host "Open Mic" episodes where listeners can talk not only with you but with each other.
- [ ] Host "Ask Me Anything" episodes where listeners can submit questions ahead of time.

WHY EVERY PODCASTER NEEDS A SEAT ON YOUTUBE

CTR Nation, let me keep it real—YouTube is today's "University of Everything." When someone wants answers, they don't just Google it—they YouTube it. If your podcast isn't there, you're leaving visibility and dollars on the table.

Plant your flag early: claim your show name on YouTube and the major socials, even if you're not posting daily yet. That handle is your digital real estate—proof that your voice exists and a beacon for future guests, clients, and sponsors who are searching right now.

When your episodes live on YouTube you unlock two game-changers:

1. **Monetization lanes**—ads, Super Thanks, memberships, brand deals.
2. **Massive discovery**—the algorithm serves your content to people who never step inside Apple or Spotify.

Give your podcast every chance to be found, funded, and celebrated. Secure those handles, upload your show to YouTube, and let the platform's global reach amplify the message God put in you. You've got this—now go press "publish."

WHY EVERY PODCASTER SHOULD CLAIM A GOOGLE BUSINESS PROFILE

Hey, CTR Fam! You know I'm all about practical visibility, so lean in for a sec. One of the simplest power moves I ever made for ***The Tina Ramsay Show*** now called ***CTR Media Network TV*** Show was grabbing a Google Business Profile (formerly "Google My Business"). Here's why you need to do the same —yesterday:

1. Instant Street Cred on the World's Biggest Search Engine
When a new listener—or a potential sponsor—types your show name into Google, you want a polished info card to pop up on the right-hand side with your artwork, link, hours, and **"Listen Now"** button. That little box shouts, "We're legit!" before anyone even clicks.

2. Map-Pin = Built-In Discovery
A Business Profile drops a pin on Google Maps. That means commuters scrolling for "business podcasts near me" can stumble onto your feed. Yes, podcasts can rank on Maps—you just have to claim the slot.

3. Review Power = Third-Party Validation
I ask every guest to leave a quick rating or—even better—a video testimonial right on my Google card. Those five-star vibes act like digital word-of-mouth. More stars ➜ more bookings ➜ more respect in the industry.

4. SEO Juice for Every Episode

Post new episodes as "Updates." Google loves fresh content, so each upload nudges your show higher in search results. Translation: free traffic from people who never open Apple or Spotify.

How to Set It Up (5-Minute Sprint)

1. Sign in to Google with the email you use for your podcast.
2. Go to business.google.com and click Add your business.
3. Enter your show name, choose Media Company/Podcast, and paste your website or host URL.
4. Verify (Google will call, text, or mail a code).
5. Add cover art, description, links, and a "Listen" button. Boom—you're live!

Pro Tips from Dr. Tina

- Ask, capture, post. After every interview, send your guest a one-line email: "Mind dropping a quick review on our Google card? Here's the link."
- Show some personality. Upload behind-the-scenes photos, short reels, and episode teasers.
- Respond to every review. It signals you value community, and Google loves active profiles.

A Google Business Profile is free, fast, and funnels fresh ears—and dollars—straight to your podcast. Pair it with your YouTube channel, and you'll own the first page of search results like a boss.

Your voice matters, and the world is Googling. Let's make sure they find you.

SCAN ME

To Start your FREE
Google My Business Page

HOW TO CREATE PODCAST SHOW NOTES THAT WORK

Show notes aren't an after-thought—they're the SEO, share-worthy, "I-need-that-link!" engine behind every episode. Use the framework below (or drop the prompts straight into ChatGPT for speed) and watch your podcast rise above the noise.

1. Magnetic Title

Give the episode a headline that stops the scroll and tells the truth.

ChatGPT Prompt: "Write ten podcast titles about [topic] that spark curiosity and promise a clear benefit." Pick the punchiest one.

2. Relatable Intro

In 2–3 lines, answer: What's this episode about? Why should the listener care?

If you have a guest, weave in a one-sentence bio that proves their credibility.

ChatGPT Prompt: "Summarize this episode on [topic + guest name] in 60 compelling words."

3. Rapid-Fire Takeaways

Bullet the top insights so busy listeners (and Google) can scan and savor. Aim for 3–7 points.

ChatGPT Prompt: "List the five most actionable takeaways from this transcript."

4. Resource Roll-Call

Drop every book, tool, or URL mentioned. Your audience gets instant value; you get extra SEO juice and affiliate clicks.

ChatGPT Prompt: "Extract all resources, links, and tools referenced in this episode."

5. Purposeful Close

Wrap it with gratitude and a clear next step: rate, subscribe, share, or grab your freebie.

ChatGPT Prompt: "Write a 40-word outro that thanks the guest and invites listeners to leave a review."

Great show notes become your episode's billboard, blog post, and backlink machine—all in one. Follow the five-part formula (or let ChatGPT draft the first pass) and turn every release into searchable, shareable gold.

Your voice matters. Let's make sure people can find it—and act on it.

HERE'S AN EXAMPLE OF HOW TO PITCH YOURSELF TO BE FEATURED ON PODCAST SHOW

Hello [Podcast Host's Name],

My name is [Your Name], and I am reaching out to you because I am a huge fan of your podcast. I've been listening to your show for some time now, and I love the valuable insights and discussions you bring to your listeners.

I am a [Your Occupation or Expertise], and I believe that I can provide valuable insights on [Topic Related to the Podcast]. I have [Briefly Mention Your Achievements or Credentials], and I am confident that I can share my expertise and add value to your show.

I understand that you are a busy person, and I appreciate the time you take to consider my request. If you think that my expertise and experiences would be a good fit for your podcast, I would be honored to be a guest on your show.

Thank you for your time and consideration, and I look forward to hearing from you soon.

Best regards,
[Your Name]

CREATE YOUR ONE PAGER LIKE THIS FOR YOUR PERSONAL BRAND

USE CANVA TO CREATE IT - SEARCH "MEDIA KIT OR ONE PAGER"

PITCHING INFLUENTIAL GUESTS: A WINNING OUTLINE

Securing high-profile guests isn't by chance—it's a repeatable system built on professionalism, personalization, and respect. Use the framework below to turn cold contacts into "Absolutely, let's do it!"

1. Lead With a One-Sheet That Wows

- Cover: show artwork + tagline
- Snapshot Stats: average downloads, top countries, biggest YouTube clip views
- Audience Avatar: who listens and why they care
- Previous Notables: three recognizable past guests or media features
- Easy Call-to-Action: "Book your episode: calendly.com/YourShow/Guest"

Pro Tip: Attach the PDF and paste a thumbnail in the email body so they see credibility at first glance.

2. Do the Homework

1. Study their latest project—book, film, startup, nonprofit.
2. Find their preferred gatekeeper (publicist, EA, or agent).
3. Note shared values—mission overlap adds instant rapport.
4. Join CTR Partner Guesting Platform

3. Craft the Irresistible Pitch (P.E.P. Formula)

Part	What to include	Example snippet
Purpose	1-line mission of your show	"We help purpose-driven founders amplify their message."
Ego Boost	Genuine, specific praise	"Your TEDx talk on conscious leadership still fuels my team's morning huddles."
Promise	Clear win for them	"Episode drops to 25K subscribers + YouTube audiogram ads targeted to your book launch city."

4. Make "Yes" Easy

- Offer two recording slots in their time zone.
- List equipment needed (just a quiet room & earbuds!).
- Include a pre-filled guest intake form—name, bio, headshot, links.

5. Respect the "No" and Nurture the "Maybe"

If they decline, reply with gratitude and a reminder that your digital door stays open. Follow up six months later with a fresh angle or milestone.

Subject: Your Conscious Leadership wisdom + 25K listeners (Guest Invite)

Hi [Name],

I'm Dr. Tina J Ramsay, host of CTR Media Network TV Show. Our mission is to spotlight leaders who turn purpose into impact. Your TEDx talk on conscious leadership still guides my production team.

Why you'll love this episode:

- 150,000K audio subscribers + 180,000K YouTube viewers in your target demographic
- Episode timed two weeks before your book launch
- We handle everything—30-minute StreamYard call; you just bring the insights.

Proposed dates: Tue 3 Oct @ 10 AM ET or Wed 4 Oct @ 2 PM ET.

One-sheet attached for quick stats and past guests. Let me know which slot works, or suggest another and we'll pivot.

Grateful for your time either way, and cheering your continued success.

Purpose-driven always,
Dr. Tina J Ramsay
Be seen, be heard, be purpose-driven.

CREATE YOUR ONE PAGER AKA MEDIA KIT FOR YOUR PODCAST

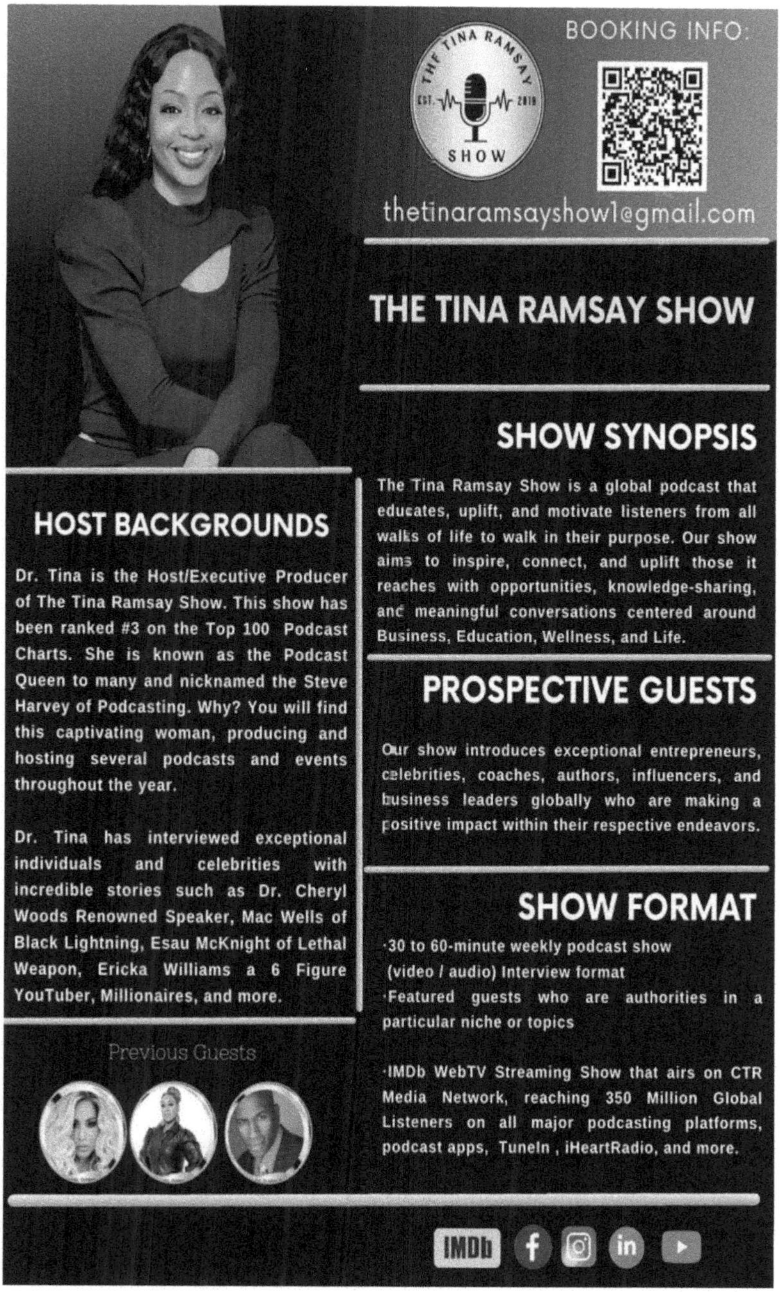

USE CANVA SEARCH "MEDIA KIT OR ONE PAGER"

HOW TO ORGANIZE YOUR PODCAST INTO SEASONS & EPISODES

Launching a podcast is the easy part; building a show that brands, sponsors, and listeners take seriously requires structure. The secret weapon? Intentional season and episode numbering. Here's my proven blueprint—straight from hosting 11 seasons of The Tina Ramsay Show now called CTR Media Network TV Show and counting.

1. Why Seasons Matter

- Professional résumé: A clean Season-by-Season archive shows potential guests and advertisers you're consistent and intentional—not a "one-and-done" hobbyist.
- Growth tracker: Season breaks let you measure downloads, tweak formats, and celebrate milestones.
- Binge-ability: New listeners love a clear starting point—"Begin at Season 3 if you're an author." That guidance keeps them hooked.

2. Choose Your Season Length

There's no podcast police, but a solid rule of thumb is 12–20 episodes per season. Long enough to deliver value; short enough to refine between seasons. If you're on fire, go longer—just label it clearly.

Dr. Tina's Reality Check: I average 20 episodes per season and drop a mini-break to regroup, monetize, and market before the next launch.

3. Two Numbering Systems (pick one and stick to it)

Number by Seasons or by seasons and episodes, or by numbering each episode. I do both ex: S11 Ep 333

3. Two Numbering Systems (pick one and stick to it)

Style	Example	Why You Might Love It	Possible "Gotchas"
Season-Only Count	*Season 3, Episode –*	Simple to say on-air (*"Welcome to Season 3!"*). Great when each season is a self-contained theme or course.	Listeners can't tell how deep your catalog is. Sponsors lose the bragging rights of a big episode number.
Dual Tag (Season + Episode)	*S5 E14*	Easiest for binge listeners to follow. Clean folders on your hard drive (*SO5_E14.wav*).	If you ever skip an episode number, fans notice.
Rolling Master Count	*Ep 333*	Shouts longevity—"Wow, 300+ episodes!"—and impresses advertisers. Motivates you as the number climbs.	A brand-new listener might feel late to the party.
Hybrid (Season + Master) *(Dr. T's pick)*	*S11 E333*	Best of both worlds: seasons for structure, big number for clout. Works beautifully in show notes and YouTube titles.	Requires discipline—update both counters every release.

4. Practical Setup Steps

1. Outline Season Goals: topic focus, guest wish-list, monetization target.
2. Batch Record Minimum 3 Episodes before airing Season 1 to stay ahead.
3. Label Audio Files "S02_E05_Title.wav" so nothing gets lost.
4. Update Artwork if a season theme shifts (fresh banner = fresh buzz).
5. Announce Finale & Kickoff Dates—build anticipation like a TV network.

Leverage Seasons for Deals

Sponsors love clear packages: "Season 4 is 15 episodes, each ad slot is $___." Guests feel honored when you say, "I'd like to feature you in our Season 5 Entrepreneur Spotlight." Order drives opportunity.

Whether you hit Episode 333 like me or reboot every 10 shows, intentional season structure proves reliability, fuels motivation, and unlocks partnerships that a scattered feed never will. Invest the time to plan—your future self (and your bank account) will thank you.

OUR 5X AWARD-WINNING BOOK & SHOW

Congratulations!

Your book "The Power of Podcasting" made it to BookAuthority's best Podcasting books of all time!

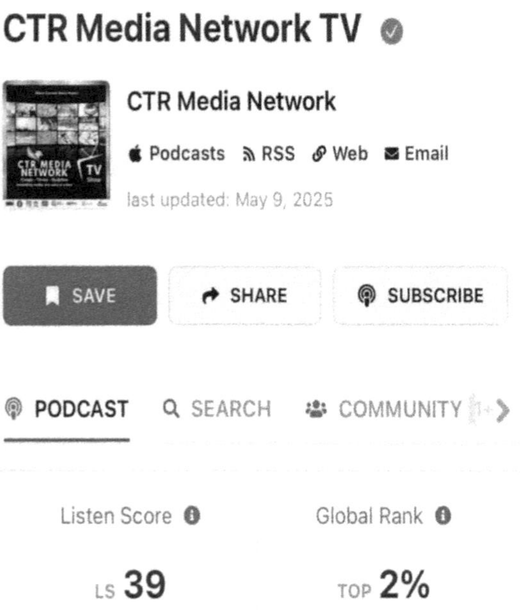

OUR SHOW NOW RANKS WITHIN THE TOP 2 % OF ALL PODCASTS GLOBALLY—OUT OF MORE THAN FIVE MILLION PODCASTS WORLDWIDE

TR MEDIA
ETWORK
ODCASTERS
IMPACTFUL
MEDIA
SUB
CTRMediaNetwork.
CTR MEDIA
NETWORK
CTR Media Network
@ctrmedianetwork
178K subscribers · 3.8K videos
More info
www.youtube.com/@ctrmedianetwork
United States
Joined Dec 6, 2020
123,168,633 views

Presented to
CTR Media Network
For passing 100,000 subscribers
YouTube

SCAN

THE GUIDE TO SOUTH CAROLINA
BUSINESS | INDUSTRY | LIFESTYLE | LEISURE
BEST OF SOUTH CAROLINA 2025
BEST OF SOUTH CAROLINA 2025
GuidetoSouthCarolina.com
CTR Media Network
Digital Marketing Firms

FOLLOW US ON SOCIAL MEDIA

Facebook
CTR Media Network

YouTube
CTR Media Network

Instagram
CTRMEDIANETWORK

LinkedIn
CTR Media Network

Google
CTR Media Network

Website
CTRMediaNetwork.com

SCAN

SCAN

SCAN

SCAN

SCAN

SCAN

References

1. The Holy Bible – Verses quoted from *the New King James Version (NKJV).*
2. Ramsay, Tina J. *The Power of Podcasting: Unlocking Tips & Strategies for Podcast Success. CTR Publishing, 2022.*
3. Ramsay, Tina J. *Visibility Is the New Currency: The CTR Media Network Guide to Marketing, Media & Monetization. CTR Publishing, 2025.*
4. Ramsay, Tina J. *CTR Wake Up and Win: 365 Days of Faith, Focus & Affirmations from Purpose-Driven Entrepreneurs & Podcasters. CTR Publishing, 2025.*
5. StreamYard Learning Videos. "StreamYard Official YouTube Channel." Accessed 2025.
6. How To Create Podcast Logo in Canva, @G-ForceNorth, YouTube Video

(All concepts, frameworks, and examples in this mini-book draw from the above sources as well as the author's personal coaching experience.)

www.ingramcontent.com/pod-product-compliance
Lightning Source LLC
LaVergne TN
LVHW050924210926
848482LV00012B/528
* 9 7 9 8 3 4 9 5 0 6 4 8 2 *